The Occult Sciences

Graphology or the Study of Handwriting

By

Various Authors

Graphology

Graphology is the analysis of the physical characteristics and patterns of handwriting. It purports to be able to identify the writer, indicate psychological state at the time of writing, and even evaluate personality characteristics. It is generally considered a pseudoscience. The word graphology comes from the Greek word 'grapho' meaning writing, and 'logos' meaning knowledge.

Jean-Charles Gille (a French psychiatrist and professor of medicine) stated in 1991 that Juan Huarte de San Juan's 1575 *Examen de ingenios para las ciencias* was the first book on handwriting analysis. In American graphology, Camillo Baldi's *Trattato come da una lettera missiva si conoscano la natura e qualita dello scrittore* (published in 1622) is considered to be the first book. Baldi's work touches on graphology more directly – and this remarkable work was rooted in the lively tradition of vernacular letter-writing manuals of sixteenth-century Italy.

It is heavily indebted to the classical Greek work *De Elocutione* (On style) attributed to Demetrius Phalereus. Baldi followed Demetrius when he condemned those whose style was too simulated, for, he says 'such people reveal nothing of themselves, all that one can tell of them is that they are shrewd and artificial.' He goes on to say that: 'when they are written without artifice or erudition or any consideration at all, but only as his nature dictates to him, then one can probably tell many things about the writer.'

Baldi only devotes a few pages to considerations of handwriting, but his insights are a significant forbear to modern graphological methods. He states 'if the writing is both fast, even and well-formed, and appears to have been written with pleasure, it has probably been written by a man who knows nothing and is worthless, because you rarely find intelligent and prudent men who write neatly... these writers are also often cold, avaricious, foolish, intemperate and indiscreet'. On the other hand he talks of writing that is 'unbecoming, crooked, badly formed and quick, yet legible'. Such writing denotes a mature man who has written a lot. Later he says 'if the handwriting is uneven, with lines that are wavy and generally ascending, such a person is naturally inclined to dominate... with such instability one can also add that he is likely to be choleric and apt to be unrestrained in following his desires.'

Around 1830 Jean-Hippolyte Michon (widely regarded as the modern father of graphology) became interested in handwriting analysis. He published his findings shortly after founding 'Société Graphologique' in 1871. The most prominent of his disciples was Jules Crépieux-Jamin (1859 - 1940) who rapidly published a series of books and analyzed and revised Michon's work – which included reclassification and re-grouping the system of 'handwriting signs.' Starting from Michon's integrative approach, Crépieux-Jamin founded a holistic approach to graphology. From the work of these two pioneers, Alfred Binet (1857 - 1911) was further convinced to conduct research into graphology from 1893 to 1907. He called it 'the science of the future' despite rejection of his results by graphologists. After World War I, interest in graphology continued to spread in Europe as well as the United States.

Although graphology had some support in the scientific community before the mid-twentieth century, more recent research rejects the validity of graphology as a tool to assess personality and job performance. In a 1987 study, graphologists were unable to predict scores on the 'Eysenck Personality Questionnaire' using writing samples from the same people. In a 1988 study, graphologists were unable to predict scores on the Myers-Briggs test using writing samples from the same people. Despite this, those in support of graphology have noted that such reports are meant to be used in conjunction with other tools, such as comprehensive background checks, practical demonstration or record of work skills. Graphology supporters state that it can complement but not replace traditional hiring tools.

Rowan Bayne, a British psychologist who has written several studies on graphology, summarized his view of the appeal of graphology: 'It's very seductive because at a very crude level someone who is neat and well behaved tends to have neat handwriting', adding that the practice is 'useless... absolutely hopeless.' The British Psychological Society ranks graphology alongside astrology, giving them both 'zero validity.' Despite this, there is some evidence of a relationship between gender and handwriting style, though the correlation is weak.

There are also objections to graphology due to perceived vagueness - for example, the German graphologist Ludwig Klages produced his findings in 1920 in, *Zeitschrift für*

Menschenkunde ('Journal for the Study of Mankind'). Klages provided a central concept, that of 'form-niveau' (or form-level): the overall level of originality, beauty, harmony, style, etc. of a person's handwriting – a quality that, according to Klages, can be perceived but not measured. According to this theory, the same sign has a positive or negative meaning depending on the subject's overall character and personality as revealed by the form-niveau. In practice, this can lead the graphologist to interpret signs positively or negatively depending on whether the subject has high or low social status. This also leads on to problems with the 'Barnum Effect' – the tendency to interpret vague statements as specifically meaningful.

Despite modern scientific opinions on graphology, it was a technique which swept over Europe in the late nineteenth and early twentieth century, with many adherents in the great letter-writing traditions of the renaissance. It provides a fascinating window into a by-gone age when handwriting was of utmost significance, now replaced by the computer and the keyboard. We hope the reader enjoys this book.

GRAPHOLOGY

I

General—Ancient and Modernised

GRAPHOLOGY is the study of the relations existing between the hand-writing of a person and his character. It is supported by observations more slender than those of Physiognomony. Its conclusions are therefore less radical, but thanks to the progress made, they are never-theless sufficiently sure for it to be classed henceforth amongst the sciences, and to be studied by people who make all possible reserves concerning the divinatory arts. And yet it has a connection with these in the sense that, by determining the tendencies which are subtly in-scribed in the written forms, it joins with them in the logical foretelling of fate and can consequently assist in the establishment of a psycho-predictive or psycho-diagnostic portrait.

Just as there are as many physiognomies as there are individuals, so there are as many kinds of writing as there are kinds of people. "And if the physiognomy," said Paul Barbe, [1] "which is so very instructive, deceives us sometimes, because it is easy to make up one's face according to the circumstances, yet the movements, which are instinctive and entirely spontaneous, cannot lead us into error."

But still it is necessary that we should have for our analysis a writing which itself is *not disguised*. Let us therefore say at once that in order to be able to form an opinion it is absolutely necessary to have before us a sincere writing, not a draft or a few words hastily written, not some writing in pencil (the pencil has not the sensitiveness of the pen), not a postcard where one is compelled to write the lines close together (the spacing between the lines, as will be seen, is of interest in graphology), not a laboured and constrained letter, sent perhaps to a superior, not the copy of a document, where the feelings of the copyist are of necessity alien to its context. The best thing is to have a letter written on *unlined paper*, written without the author knowing

---

[1] *Telle ecriture, tel caractère* (Jules Rouff, publisher).

that it would be studied from the point of view with which we are dealing, a letter written spontaneously and in such a manner that it truly reflects the natural state of mind of its author.

In any case the fact that a writing is disguised does not escape the acute expert. For even if the shape habitually given to the letters is falsified, or their slope (by making upright a usually slanting writing) is altered, yet some details will soon disclose the fraud to the practised graphologist, and he will, and with good reason, not express an opinion on this dishonest disguise, any more than a physiognomist would give an opinion as to the true expression of an actor on the stage.

What is the use of Graphology ? Even if it were only to give you information as to the person from whom you receive a letter, whether on business, from a new friend, distant relative, or desired object of our love, would it not be a great boon to know something of his temperament, to guess his tendencies, so as to be put on our guard or to accept his sympathy ? But there is more than this, we repeat—to guess the temperament of a person, does it not mean foreseeing what he will do, what may happen to him, what the future has in store for him ?

Having said this, let us recall in a few lines that from the earliest times the appearance of the handwriting struck prudent people. With them it was but intuition, and the reasoned study of writing was not to be started till our century. But Aristotle already claimed that he could define the soul of people by their way of writing, and when Suetonius noticed that the Emperor Augustus did not separate his words, he came to the conclusion that he neglected the detail for the sake of the vast whole. Later Goethe became much interested (in what subject was this great genius not interested ?) in these psychological curiosities. As early as 1622 Camillo Baldi wrote a small Latin book about them called *De Signis ex Epistolis.* Lavater studied them. The German Heuze erected a system on which unfortunately he committed nothing to writing.[1]

The true promoter of scientific Graphology is the Abbé Michon[2] a preacher and novelist of Corrèze (1806 to 1881), and the first serious book on the subject is that which he published in collaboration with Desbarolles.[3]

Since then important books have been published by Crépieux-Jamin,[4] Varinard,[5] Raymond,[6] R. de Salberg,[7] A. de Rochetal,[8]

---

[1] In 1915 a small book was published without author's name, but attributed to Hocquart : *The Art of Judging Characters of Men by their Writing,* full of original sketches.

[2] We must not, however, forget that as early as 1830 the Abbé Flandrin began to systematise graphology after long studies in the Library of Autographs.

[3] *The Mysteries of Writing.*

[4] *Treatise of Graphology.*—Writing and Character.

[5] *Course of Graphology.*

[6] *Man is in his Writing,* preface by Elie Dautrin.

[7] *Manual of Common Graphology.*

[8] *Graphology Put Within the Reach of All.*

etc., and numerous popular works. Graphological studies are likewise found in the general books on the divinatory arts, such as the one by Jules de Grandpré. [1]

And all are agreed that there is a close connection between the different parts of the body, that they are animated by the same mind. It is the body which produces the arm, the arm the hand, the hand the fingers. All movements receive their impulse from the mind (we mean by this for the moment temperament, character), and it follows that the mind reveals itself in the movement. And among all movements there are none so varied as those of the hand and the fingers.

And does not the same phenomenon lead us to similar conclusions in art ?

Does not the temperament of a painter reveal itself in his pictures ? Some occultists even claim that it would be possible to deduce from the pictures of a painter not only his character but also his physique, that the elegance of Raphael, the strength of Rubens, the clear brown complexion of Holbein, the ruddy face of Largillère are found in their work. The brush also is a pen which indicates the man.

And after all what is writing but a drawing ? A drawing which speaks. And what it says has two meanings, the meaning deliberately put into the context, and the meaning unconsciously put into the outward shape of the context, that is to say the graphism.

Before passing on to practical graphology, let us relate some anecdotes which show the usefulness of this beautiful science.

Here is one which comes from the Memoirs of the Comte Horace de Viel Castel, that evil but witty tongue of the reign of Napoleon III.

At the time of the betrothal of Mlle. de Duras with the Marquis de Custine, the Duchess de Duras had one day in her drawing room the young couple, the Comte de Nieuwerkerke, Baron Humboldt and a few other guests. Graphology was talked about, and Humboldt claimed that he could from the writing of people recognise their character. The Duchess suddenly handed him a letter and asked what he thought of the writer.

Our scientist looks, examines, thinks, and begins to hold forth. He shows point by point that the author of the letter can only be bizarre, corrupt, of whom in short he drew an atrocious portrait without noticing that the Duchess, much annoyed, tried all she could to interrupt, or at least to soften the merciless verdict which dealt with the aspiring Marquis himself—who was present at the charge !

The marriage was broken off. Custine married Mlle. de Courtomer and became the sad type whom everyone knows. The solemn German had not made a mistake.

---

[1] *The Art of Predicting the Future* (Fayard, publisher). Any desired documentation on this particular art will also be found in the *History of Graphology* of Émilie de Vars.

THE OCCULT SCIENCES

M. Michon tells how he was asked by a worthy man aged 40 to examine his writing, in which the famous Abbé discovered an excessive melancholy, obvious loyalty, but also a heartrending lack of energy. His correspondent wanted his opinion, being on the one hand a bachelor very anxious to marry a certain young lady of 25 with whom he was much in love, and being on the other hand obsessed with the desire to go to Paris and start in business. The graphologist did not fail to advise him to give up his commercial intentions, as he was too naïf and not sufficiently strong willed, and also to abandon his matrimonial plans relating to a woman who was too young and whom he would make unhappy. The good man took the advice, being thus saved from the double risk of compromising his fortune and his domestic happiness.

A police officer friend of ours owed to Graphology one of the successes of his career. Some money had been stolen in a house, and no clue made the finding of the culprit possible. Having however noticed some blotting paper on which a note, not signed, had been blotted, and the master and mistress of the house having stated that they had had no opportunity of writing for three days, he examined the few lines written by reading them on the spot in a looking-glass, and described the probable character of the writer; the description corresponded with the son who, on being questioned, became troubled and finally with tears admitted his theft and the name of the young woman for whose pleasure he had committed it, and with whom he had just fixed up a meeting to bring her the proceeds.

In conclusion let us be ultra-modern and copy this extract from a newspaper of the 15th April, 1925 :—

> " Let us watch our writing ! This obviously becomes necessary now that several American Life Assurance Societies refuse to decide the premium to be paid on death before having a specimen of the writing of the assured.
>
> Dr. Broud Kurt, who was the promoter of this new decision, claims that their clients must be divided into three classes, according to the size of the letters which they write.
>
> Those in group 1 will disappear nine years after the signing of their policies, those of the second group 25 years after, and those of the third group 50 years after.
>
> Figures given haphazard, you say ? In principle one might be inclined to believe it. But what is exceedingly disturbing is that statistics drawn up from the assured who have died proved Dr. Kurt entirely right."

II

Method

Some graphologists have tried to analyse the whole of the alphabet *letter by letter,* both as to the capitals and the small letters. This method has the double defect of being too fastidious and too detailed. It proves badly by wanting to prove too much. The more so as the same person, even sincerely, forms the same letters differently in the course of a page. In this Encyclopædia where we guard against charlatanism, giving facts and ideas only by way of reference and with all reserve, we maintain that in Graphology as in all the other arts called divinatory we must exaggerate nothing; that it is better to find in it only hints, sometimes very sure, but sometimes also somewhat vague, which must be taken into consideration only so far as they appear to corroborate each other.

We think therefore that in Graphology it is necessary and sufficient to study :—

1. The general appearance of the writing.
2. The appearance of the letters.
3. The secondary appearances (dots, lines, terminations, paragraphs, etc.).
4. The influences which may modify the writing (health, age, nationality, etc.).

It is under these four heads that we shall divide our remarks, giving or adding to them synoptic forms. And in this connection also let us note that if these tables are convenient, they run the risk of having a kind of dogmatic look against which we warn the reader. He must remember that other signs may seem to contradict them ; here also, therefore, it is an *average* which we have to look for, according to the great occult law of results.

Before going fully into the subject, two words more, as to the *graphic signs* and as to the *style* of the writer.

A graphic sign may be simple, for instance the return hook of the M. It may also be complex, if for instance this hook, already significant, is in addition club shaped.

The more frequent and well defined a sign is, the more intensity it reveals in the quality or the defect which it expresses.

Generally speaking, each writing has one or more dominants. It is well to be able to ascertain them. Often they jump to the eye and form a guide for the remainder of the researches.

In the same way the quality of the style, clear or confused, frank or reticent, the syntax, the spelling, enable us at once to see if we are dealing with an ignorant or an educated person, a frank or an insincere being, an intelligent man or an idiot. This is not yet pure graphology, but no one would deny that this preliminary study prepares for it by giving the judgment hints for its subsequent examination.

The following is a table of results drawn up by J. Crépieux-Jamin :–

		RESULTS
The " t " weakly crossed	Weak will	} Cowardice.
Large lines of the pen	Imagination	
Very sloping writing	Great sensitiveness	} Lack of judgment.
Large lines of the pen	Imagination	
Upward lines	Ardour.	
Short endings	Economy	} Love of gambling.
Restless writing	Agitation	
Sloping letters	Sensitiveness	
Clear and harmonious writing	Clear intellect	
Rapid writing	Quick ideas	} Penetration.
Writing barely sloping	Moderate sensitiveness	
Very sloping writing	Sensitiveness	} Balanced sensitiveness.
Closed angles	Firmness.	
Sober writing	Approbation	
Harmonious writing	Intelligence	} Slight vanity.
Rising writing	Ardour, ambition	
Writing very sloping	Sensitiveness	} Lack of positivism (weathercock).
Letters close together	Intuition	
Curves	Gentleness	
" N " written like " U "	Benevolence	} Devotion.
Writing sloping a little	Sensitiveness	
Writing very sloping	Sensitiveness	} Laziness and unhappiness.
" T " not crossed	Lack of will-power	
Rounded writing	Gentleness	
Serpentine writing	Supple mind	
Words getting smaller	Delicacy	} Theft and lying.
Backhand writing	Dissimulation	
Re-entering hooks	Egoism	
Very sloping writing	Passion	} Injustice.
Long " T " crossing	Liveliness	
Very sloping writing	Sensitiveness	} Susceptibility.
Sign of self-satisfaction.	Vanity	
Re-entering hooks	Egoism	
" T " crossing sword shaped	Satire	} Spite.
Signs of pride	Pride	
Rounded lines	Gentleness, weakness	} Lack of conscience.
Very sloping writing	Sensitiveness, passion	

GRAPHOLOGY

RESULTS

Quiet writing	Quiet mind	} Patience.
Rounded writing	Gentleness	
Light and graceful writing ..	Delicacy	} Timidity.
Sloping writing.	Sensitiveness	
" T " weakly crossed ..	Weak will-power ..	
" T " crossed long	Vivacity	} Spitefulness.
Sloping writing	Sensitiveness	
Fine writing	Impotence	
" T " crossed long	Impotence	} Very bad temper.
Sloping writing	Vivacity	
Heavy writing or with thick strokes	Strength	
Words getting smaller ..	Delicacy	} Diplomacy.
Serpentine writing.	Suppleness of mind ..	

III

General Appearance of Writing

This appearance relates to :—

(a) The margination ;
(b) The direction and the spacing of the lines ;
(c) The spacing of the letters and the words ;
(d) The height of the letters ;
(e) The movement, the clearness, the legibility of the writing ;
(f) The joining of the letters between each other, and even of the words to each other.

(a) The margination of a page is the first thing which strikes the eye, but too great importance must not be attached to it.

No doubt graphologists tell us that a page without margins or paragraphs indicates avarice ; an equal margin both sides, nicely framing the page, indicates order and harmony ; a normal and regular margin on one side only denotes economy ; a very wide one, generosity ; an increasing one, extravagance overcoming economy ; a decreasing one, economy overcoming extravagance.

But we must not exaggerate, and above all we must avoid somewhat too easy deductions. We see people writing now with a margin, now without, according to whether they have little or much to say.

We prefer putting our faith in the appearance, whether clean or neglected, sometimes dirty, of the paper and the envelope. This certainly indicates the care or otherwise which the writer bestows on what he does. Spots, blotches, a sheet with a corner turned down are not very flattering signs.

One observation : look rather at the end of the letter than at its beginning on which generally more care is bestowed. The end gives a closer knowledge of the writer ; and if the writing, good at the start, becomes scrawling, you may be sure that you are dealing with a nervy or impatient person, who is apt to lack an orderly mind and persever-ance.

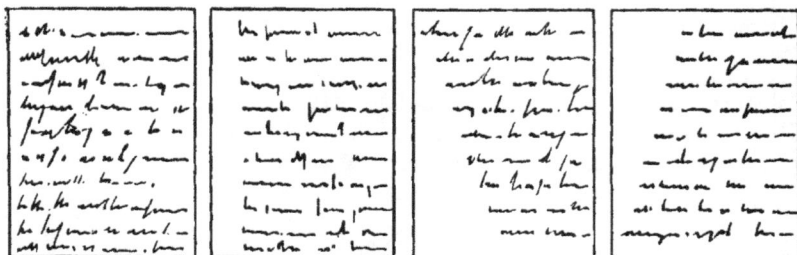

MARGINS.

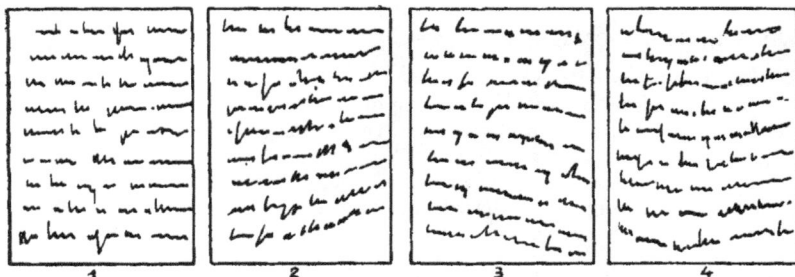

1   2   3   4

LINES.

(b) The direction of the lines is much studied by graphologists.

1. A horizontal, rigid, straight writing denotes will-power, inflexi-bility.

The same, without too much rigidity—uprightness and persever-ance.

The same, soft—weak will-power, hesitation, irresolution.

2. A writing sloping upwards belongs to him who has dash and ambition.

Sloping upwards but sloppy, it means stupid vanity.

If it climbs, it is no longer ambition, but exaltation.

3. A writing sloping downwards is a sign of pessimism, of melancholy.[1]

If it topples down in some way, the pessimism becomes mournfulness, gloominess.

And if, sloping downwards, it yet shews some signs of strength, there is danger of discouragement, even of suicide.

4. A writing with concave lines denotes reaction against adversity, an effort to fight against fate.

A writing with convex lines shews presumption, with easy ups and downs.[2]

A sinuous serpentine writing—suppleness of mind, diplomacy.[3]

But of course it is possible for these various signs to be combined.

The spaces between the lines also have their value :—

> Clear and regular—sane judgment.
> Irregular—imagination predominating.
> Very close—avarice.
> Very wide—liberality.

For ourselves we do not think it necessary to place too much reliance on this. Narrow spaces between lines may mean an abundance of ideas desired to be incorporated in one page. Wide spaces mean not so much liberality of the purse as liberality of the mind.

(c) The same remark applies to the spacing of the letters. It may be that a close writing denotes avarice ; but in the end if this sign is to be found, it must be as the result of all the graphic close spacings—letters, lines and spaces between lines. And even then do not let us be too much in a hurry !

According to this means of observation we find :—

> Widely spaced letters—prodigal instincts.
> Wide spaces with long end letters—generosity.
> Widely spaced letters without hooks (a sign of egoism)—disinterestedness.
> Widely spaced letters with hooks—interested generosity.
> Widely spaced letters with large strokes of the pen—extravagance.
> Normally spaced letters—wise economy.

Close writing must not be mistaken for small writing. Besides it is possible to make small writing with large letters.

---

[1] Dr. Schwiedland gives the following physiological reason, Being discouraged, tired, we lean towards less fatiguing movements, towards letting the arm drop. On the other hand the optimist is brave, and not afraid of the effort which " in some way raises his hand and makes the writing slope upwards."

[2] For instance Mme. de Pompadour—constant but ineffectual effort. And she died young.

[3] Diplomacy, according to Crépieux-Jamin, is the result, rather than the sign, of delicacy and suppleness.

(*d*) In children's writing the letters usually get larger towards the end of the word ; it has been noticed that in them, and also in grown-ups, it is a sign of childishness.

It follows that a gladiolated writing (sword-shaped, that is to say getting smaller towards the end of the word) is a sign of the opposite —cunning. And if the end of the words is sometimes illegible because so small, or is merely a wavy line, we are entitled to think that the cunning becomes dissimulation, even perfidy.

Writing of medium height and regular in this respect denotes integrity, loyalty.

Irregular medium writing—versatility.

Writing getting larger and heavy—obstinacy, exaggeration.

Writing getting larger, but light—simplicity, credulity.

Writing getting larger and inharmonious—stupidity.

(*e*) The *movement* of the writing is in our opinion a subtle but sure indication.

An excited person writes quickly, for vivacity is of the essence of his movements.

A calm man writes steadily. And this is recognised at once.

A hasty and very quick writing—extreme activity.

If it is only quick, lack of reflection may be feared.

If it is merely brisk, it resembles the mind, active and ready.

The writing may also breathe strength, health. Then it is called dynamogenious.

The calm writing of which we spoke above may be soft like the writer.

Careless writing indicates thoughtlessness ; if hesitating, indecision ; if trembling, fatigue. But here we fall into too easy assimilations.

Much to be preferred is the information conveyed by a clear and distinct writing, the daughter of mental balance, to that conveyed by a confused, tangled, in one word bizarre, writing, the daughter of an odd mind.

Legibility may be rapid and easy in frank, brisk and honest characters.

It may also exist, but slow like their thought, which accentuates the sign of honesty.

Illegible but equal—an ardent, precipitate, impulsive nature.

Illegible but pointed, the words getting smaller—cunning, dissimulation, inscrutability.

(*f*) The joining of letters and words gives information to the graphologist from the psychological standpoint that the intuitive creator of ideas puts these down without connection, whereas the deductive type carries out, deduces, reasons, hence connects.

From this point of view we therefore have two kinds of writing, the detached, cut, and the connected. If we raise this observation to the ethnographical level, so as to give it a striking confirmation, we find that the Oriental who is contemplative, has a detached writing, and that the Occidental, who is practical, and acts, has a connected writing.

The following are the main differences in this graphological scheme :

A writing entirely disconnected denotes a taste for paradox—if less so, a taste for theorising, intuition.

If only the first letter of the word is disconnected—intuition followed by realisation. [1]

The connected writing, as we have said, belongs to the deductive type.

If even the words are joined together—excess of deductiveness, sophistry.

Writing with an equal number of letters disconnected and an equal number connected—good mental balance.

More letters detached than connected—ideas predominate.

Less letters detached than connected—realisation predominates.

IV

Appearance of the Letters (*Capitals*)

The simplest means of making ourselves understood would seem to be to draw up a table :—

1. Simple capitals, well traced, or resembling small letters—well developed intellect.

2. Ungraceful and awkward capitals—poor intellect.

3. Graceful capitals, with harmonious curves descending below the line—taste, elegance, æsthetic sense.

4. Capitals resembling print—æsthetic sense, love of form.

5. Capitals with many flourishes and curves—pretension, ostentation.

6. Capitals resembling figures—methodical people who reason from exact premises.

7. Dashing capitals—trenchant characters.

8. Capitals very long as compared with the following small letters—pride. Capitals low and small—modesty or dissimulation.

---

[1] " In writings which have all the letters connected, there are some which have the first letter cleanly disconnected, and I have found that this sign corresponded with brains rich in deductiveness, but which yet had an initial movement towards intuition " (Abbé Michon).

9. Capitals closely written —timidity. Capitals very large and open —bluff.

10. Capitals large at foot—practical sense. Capitals large on the top—idealism or vanity.

11. Capitals high up " as if on stilts "—self-sufficiency, vanity.

12. Capital underlining the following letters—self-complacency. Capital covering the following letters—protecting pride.

13. Capital ending towards the left—fight with oneself. Capital ending towards the right—independent spirit.

14. Very large capitals—pretentiousness. Absence of capitals, modesty or material mind.

15. Hook at beginning—acquisitiveness. Hook at both ends—avarice.

16. Capital ending in backward hook—egoism. Capital connected with the small letter following—self-forgetfulness.

The letter M in particular attracts attention by its variations :—

17. The M with three downstrokes, called aristocratic, denotes a person of the cultured world. The M with two downstrokes, called popular, denotes the contrary, or if it is found among. intellectuals, all failures write it thus. If very high and very broad—boasting, self-confidence.

18. The first downstroke higher than the others—pride of comparison. Downstrokes equal size—no ambition. If like the last—desire for approval.

19. Like a down staircase—pessimism. Like an upward staircase —vulgar ambition.

20. Joining of strokes rounded, angular, or half-way up :—1, Gentleness ; 2, Obstinacy ; 3, Keen acquisitiveness.

V

Appearance of the Letters—Small

We propose to study them from the following points of view :—

Dimensions, direction, shape, arrangement and plastic, openness, soberness, slope, upstrokes and downstrokes.

A. Writing wide—courage, openness, daring.
        ,,   sinuous and supple—the parvenu.
        ,,   rigid and firm—great daring.
        ,,   high and upright—pride, even arrogance.
        ,,   high and sloping—compassionate pride.
        ,,   high with backward hooks—pride, disdain.
        ,,   narrow—timidity if it is high ; or avarice if it is small and compact.

GRAPHOLOGY

Writing not wide but high—largeness of views, knowledge of one'
    own strength.
    „   high and wide—love of display.
    „   high and narrow—constraint.
    „   high and alert—great imagination.
    „   high and slow—proud aspirations.
    „   small—cunning, minutia, sometimes avarice.
    „   small and harmonious—delicacy of mind.
    „   small and harmonious, the crossing of the " T " ending in
        point—caustic character.
    „   small and harmonious with last letter ending in a point—
        cunning.
    „   small and inharmonious—stinginess.
    „   small and inharmonious with regular pointing—mania.
    „   small and inharmonious, close and compact—avarice.
    „   small, low and flat—timid humility, no breadth of mind.

But it must not be forgotten that long-sighted people write large
and short-sighted people small. Therefore, before coming to a decision.
we must study other graphological elements.

A thick writing denotes material instincts, greediness, sensuality.

A thin writing denotes an absence of voluptuousness.

A firm writing shows energy and temperament.

But firm and defaced—coarseness, brutality.

A light writing (less firm than the thin) denotes delicacy, weakness,
a somewhat sickly nature.

B. Let us pass on to the direction of the letters. It is based on the
distinction between the strong, the active, the go-ahead and the hesitating, the delaying in everything. The former have been called
dextrogyrous and the latter sinistrogyrous, because the former slope
their writing towards the right, the others towards the left or backwards.

If a dextrogyrous writing slopes towards the right strokes which
should normally slope towards the left, this denotes in its author
activity, intelligence, altruism.

If on the other hand a sinistrogyrous writing slopes towards the
left strokes intended for the right, we infer from this that its author
is slow, hesitating, inactive. Thus the head of a business will know
beforehand the character of him who applies for a post by letter.

C. Shape. This is either rounded or angular.

A rounded writing denotes an easy temper, gentleness, sometimes
softness and indecision.

Rounded and very sloping—passion leading perhaps to a lack of
conscience.

Rounded, sloping and connected—self-abandonment.

Rounded, sloping and upward—devotion.

Rounded, sloping and calm—patience, and in the case of soft writing, laziness.

An angular writing indicates a peevish obstinate character.

If it is angular and sloping—weak sentimentality.

Angular, erect and alert—quarrelsome mind.

Angular, erect and stiff—malevolence.

There are writings which are so to speak square—they can bend, but rule if necessary.

D. There are also orderly careful writings. Others are disorderly and scrawling. And they are so consistently or intermittently, indicating constancy or inconstancy of instinct.

Needless to say a " made " handwriting has no graphological value. But there are pleasing, beautiful, harmonious writings, indicating good taste, and unpleasant, ugly inharmonious writings which indicate the contrary.

E. We do not think too much ought to be made of the openness of letters (a, o, g, q, etc.), of which the gamut is as follows :—

Letters very open—thoughtless confidence, indiscretion.

„ open at the top—expansiveness, frankness.

„ open backward—expansiveness towards strangers.

„ open at the bottom—hypocrisy, dishonesty.

„ open irregularly—discretion.

„ generally closed—reserve.

„ hermetically closed—inscrutability.

„ with curves—concentration.

„ with curves above—open backwards—hypocritical expansiveness.

F. Graphologists also claim to read in the soberness or the flourishes, in the one a sign of gravity, in the other a sign of vanity, going as far as coquetry or silliness. A dry writing denotes a sense of truth and the abstract. Severity makes a writing dry, angular and rigid.

G. The slope of the writing gives the following shades :—

Sloping backwards—dissimulation, reserve, distrust.

Upright—strength of character and judgment.

Sloping very slight—sensitiveness of the heart, but calm maintained.

Well sloping—tenderness, the heart dominating the head.

Very sloping—almost lying down—excessive sensitiveness.

Varied sloping—struggle between the heart and the head.

H. The downstrokes and upstrokes have been the subject matter of various observations :—

    Rounded and slight—tenderness.
    Rounded and thick—devotion.
    Angular and light—egoism, dryness of heart.
    Angular and thick—coarse passion.
    Upper downstroke larger than lower—intellectual activity.
    Lower downstroke larger than upper—physical activity.
    Downstrokes well proportioned—mental and physical balance.
    Tail of downstroke curved—sprightliness.
    Downstrokes short—clear mind and sane judgment.
           ,,   long—lively imagination.
           ,,   excessively long—exalted imagination.
           ,,   crossed—obstinacy.
           ,,   with curves or little hooks at bottom—verbiage.
    Downstroke connected with the small letter following—sociability.

The small **D**, like the capital **M**, has attracted special attention. It has all sorts of shapes, of which the following are the principal :—

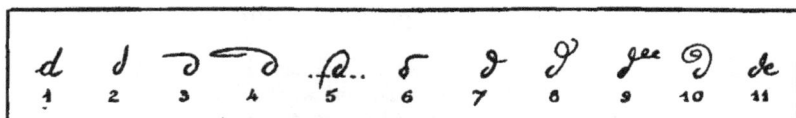

1. Copybook type—simplicity, even insignificance.
2. Going straight up—ideal aspirations.
3. Inclined to the left—intellectuality.
4. Covering the preceding letters—struggle against imagination.
5. Going below the line—egoism.
6. Thrown forward to the right—independence.
7. With right hand curve—imagination.
8. Curved with stroke across—lively imagination.
9. With repeated curves—exaltation.
10. With flourishes—coquetry, pretentiousness.
11. Connected with the following small letter—sequence of ideas.

     .   .   .   .

We repeat once more with Mr. Barbe himself—graphologists have multiplied the signs to such an extent that in the end they have spoilt the interest in the signs. Each new expert tries to find something fresh. Let us be careful. We will, however, give the chief discoveries recently made or claimed to have been made, and we shall close our study of the small letters. Here again a table would be convenient :—

GRAPHOLOGY

1. Greek letters—some vanity.
2. Small " b " with convex back—benevolence.
3. Letters finished afterwards—love of detail.
4. Curves descending below the line—keenness for money.
5. The " m " and the ' n " curved at top—firm character.
6. The same letters curved at the bottom—gentleness, amiability.
7. The letters " p," " j " etc., taller than the other letters—clear imagination.
8. The " j," " g," etc., crossed in the middle of the downstroke—domestic tyranny.
9. The " v " going up a little higher than the following letter—sense of duty.
10. The " x " like a St. Andrew's cross, with straight lines—fighting spirit.

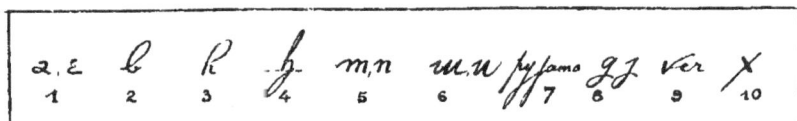

Let us stop here so as not to get fanciful.   And rather, returning to the main line of our observations, let us say that the general appearance gives excellent indications, much better than these too precise details.

Yes, it is correct that the courageous man, with broad and daring gestures, will have a writing of the same kind, that the timid man, who makes himself small in his life, will write closely, that a person with broad views will have a tall writing, whereas the meticulous will cling to the details of a writing which will almost always be very small. It is correct that a broad writing denotes appetites, and that a fine writing marks delicacy, etc.

In the same way there are writings which reveal clearness, frankness or dissimulation, aristocratic and common writings, etc.   It seems to us that we must not try to go too far in reading a soul with certainty through some shape of a letter or other sign.   This might lead us into mistakes, and by insisting on it into charlatanism.

VI

Secondary or Accessory Appearances of Writing

These consist of the accents, the crossings, the dots and the punctuation, the initials and finals, the signatures and flourishes, the erasures.

A. It is logical, if not always correct, to say that order shews itself in placing accents regularly, but the contrary may be the result of mental super-activity.

Accents placed rather high suggest good activity; those which are heavy and placed low indicate less high instincts.

The accent with a hook would indicate a restless mind. The circumflex accent drawn in one line betokens mental activity.

B. The logical double dash framing a secondary phrase indicates a cultured person.

Too many words underlined attract the eye with an annoying presumption.

The crosses of the T have been much observed on account of their amazing variety, and the following table has been drawn up :—

Length :—

    None (that is absence of cross)—ill-will.
1. Weak—mediocre will power.
2. Long—vivacity, impatience.
    Normal—good will.

Resemblance :—

    Dissimilar in the same writing—inconstancy.
    Cross always alike—constant will-power.

Height :—

3. The cross low—submissive character.
    Half way up—calm thoughtful will.
    Rather high—strong will.
4. Above the " t "—domineering character.
5. Making a curve above the " t "—oppressive will.

Thickness :—

6. Fine—vivacity of mind.
7. Strong—strong will.
8. Heavy—violent temperament.
9. Thicker at one end—coarse instincts.

Place :—

10. Behind the " t "—hesitation.
    Crossing the " t "—decision.
11. In front of the " t "—initiative.

Shape :—

12. Very thick at the end—powerful will.
13. Very thick at the beginning—enthusiasm.
14. Getting thinner—aggressive will.
15. Like a harpoon at the end and upward—supple tenacity.
16. Like a harpoon at the end and downward—tenacity without suppleness.
17. Like a harpoon at the beginning, tenacious resistance.

Direction :—

18. Rising at an angle from the bottom—contradictory mind.
19. Rising from the middle—disputing mind.
20. Rising in a curve—unaggressive quibbling mind.
21. Rising in a rigid line—aggressive quibbling mind.
22. Going down in a rigid line—obstinacy.

Curved lines :—

23. Concave curve—gentle cheerfulness.
24. Curve thicker in the middle—love of material pleasures.
25. Curve like a whiplash—carelessness.
26. Curve like a lasso—seductive will-power.

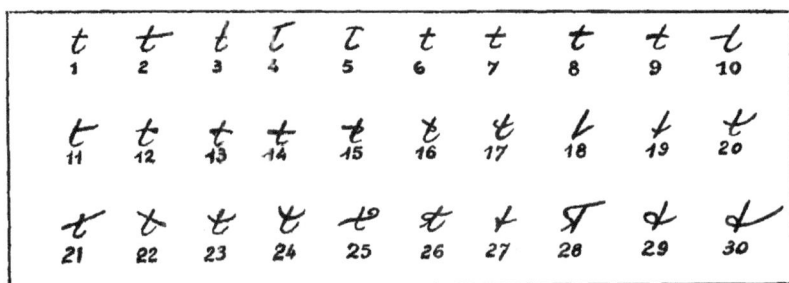

Backward curves :—

27. Angular—obstinacy.
28. Angular and long—strong obstinacy.
29. Ending at the bottom in a curve—patience.
30. Returning curve and long—pigheadedness.

These types of crossings are simple. But in most cases the writing shows various combinations of these types. It is for the expert graphologist to find a solution.

C. There is a very old saying—putting the dots on the " i's," which means, be exact. The dot on the " i " has become a graphological element which has the following variations :—

Absence of dots—negligence.
Dots placed regularly and well—careful orderly mind.
Dot to the right of the " i "—quick mind.
Dot to the left of the " i "—slow thinking.
Light dot placed high—imagination, even mysticism.
Light dot placed low—practical even earthly mind.
Dot accentuated—firmness, sensuality.

Point lengthening into an accent—ardent nature.
Thick and heavy dot—coarse instincts.
Dot like a light comma—mental activity.
Dot like a heavy comma—diligent mind.
Square thick dot—materialism.
Point connected with the following small letter—great enthusiasm.

So much for the dot crowning the " i." [1] Now for the dot ending the sentences :—

If it is always lacking—lack of distrust.
If it follows the signature—distrust.
Heavy or light—materialism or spiritualism.

Punctuation likewise gives information :—

Correct punctuation—order and logic.
Bad punctuation—intellectual activity and lack of distrust.
Light or heavy exclamation mark—spiritualism or materialism.
Repeated exclamation mark—enthusiasm.
Graceful and light question mark—æsthetic taste.
Heavy and badly made question mark—lack of taste.
Repeated question mark—mental exaltation.
Dots or dashes—if they are all over the place—romanticism.

D. Study of first and last letters of words :—

1. Small hook at the beginning of a capital—acquisitiveness.
Curve like the handle of basket—reserve and concentration.
Large initial curve—dash, gaiety.
Rigid line at the start—combativeness and even contradictoriness.
2. Last letter cut short, medium or long—economy, wisdom, extravagance.
Rising, curved—religiosity, gratitude.
Rising stiff—susceptibility, temper.
Horizontal—affection, courtesy.
Descending—practical mind.
Drooping—keenness for money.
Turning to the left—self-conflict.
Last letter thickening upward—strong will.
Last letter forming an acute angle—peevishness.
Last letter like a rising harpoon—supple tenacity.
Last letter like a falling harpoon—tenacity without diplomacy.
Last letter curved—gentleness.
Very large last letter—exaltation, ostentation.
Last letter flying into the air—quibbling.

[1] Albert de Rochetal, editor of the *Graphological Review*, is amongst those for whom the dots on the " i " have much importance. In his book (*Graphology Put Within the Reach of All*) he says that the accentuation of a dot is the accentuation of an idea.

E. The signature in our opinion has much more value than the majority of the other graphological signs.[1] It is a very sure sign of personality—it becomes its seal. Hence the number of types of signatures and flourishes is enormous; there are almost as many as there are persons. Yet they have been classified (see table with figures given).

A signature without flourish belongs to mediocrity; but if it is that of an intellectual person it reveals a superior being to whom his

name suffices because it contains the whole of him. Many men of genius and high position, rulers of the mob, have neglected the flourish. For instance Corneille, Victor Hugo.

1. A signature followed by a dot denotes a prudent cautious nature, afraid of opinion. For instance the signature of Thiers.

2. A signature followed by a stroke denotes the distrustful man who is on his guard and plays all his trumps. For instance Mirabeau.

3. A signature ending in a downward stroke like a sword betokens

---

[1] From the commercial, judicial, anthropometrical point of view, says Professor Raymond, the signature is of the greatest importance, and therefore could not be missed by Graphology Without this peculiarity the whole economic life would suffer; it is the talisman against forgers, and he who ventures to forge a signature carries his condemnation in his own hand.

the defensive type. If the end is like a club, the resolute defensive ; if like a harpoon, violently defensive.

4. A flourish after the signature ending in a point denotes the aggressively militant (Robespierre). Yatagan-shaped—the combative fighter (Henri Rochefort). Vertical or almost—brain predominant (Pasteur), with signs of will-power if it thickens, of combativeness if it gets thinner, of tenacity if like a harpoon, etc.

5. The shield-like flourish (seeming to protect the name and then drooping) denotes the courageous, but with a shade of prudence.

6. A plain line underlining the name—pride of one's own personality (Barrès).

7. A back stroke without curve—defensive, grudge-bearing.

8. Stroke underlining with little hook at end—pride mixed with skill.

9. Back stroke with several angular return lines—energetic vindictive fighter.

10. Backstroke like lightning or zigzag—active and quick self-willed.

If the zigzags are rounded or angular—gentleness or rigidity in such will-power.

11. The back stroke forming gentle curves is that of the cheerful type, of the good-natured.

12. Lasso with several knots—great skill (F. Arago).

If the lassos cross each other—divided from the signature—spirit of intrigue.

13. If the lasso takes the shape of a corkscrew—cunning.

14. The flourish like a knotted necktie is that of tact, of skill in negociations.

15. A cobwebby flourish—industrial or commercial ability.

A flourish like railings—distrust.

16. A flourish almost completely surrounding the name tells of an egotism which insists on satisfaction.

If the flourish completely surrounds the name and encloses it— the life is neither expansive nor bright.

VII

Summary

Many have tried to *sum up* the art of Graphology, to prepare convenient tables. F. Clerget gave quite a good summary in a little book called *How to Read in the Thought*. Here it is, agreeing roughly with the detailed data which we have given :—

GRAPHOLOGY

Writing.—Accentuated—despotism. Lengthy—suppleness. Angular—strength, energy. Sloping—ambition, dash. Well spaced—method, order, judgment. Curved—weakness, gentleness. Downward—discouragement, melancholy. Hard to read—dissimulation. Like strokes of a sword—ardour, courage, struggle. Wide—extravagance. Narrow—meanness. Firm—integrity, loyalty. Fine and close—carefulness, cunning, avarice. Strong—passion. Getting smaller—cunning. Getting thicker—frankness, naivety. Sloping—sensitiveness. Connected—calculation. Masterly—nobility. Neglected—thoughtlessness, carelessness, laziness. Clear—order, method. Sloping from right to left—feeling. Sloping from left to right—resistance, revolt. Straight—reason. Small—carefulness. Large—will-power, domination. Without end letters—economy. Serpentine—cunning, lies. Thin—discretion, reserve. Level—calm, tranquillity.

Lines.—Sloping upwards—ambition. Sloping downwards—discouragement. Sloping upwards and downwards—unequal character. Straight—order, calm. Wide spaced—extravagance. Incoherent—restlessness, agitation. Many on the page—economy, churlishness. Wavy—cunning, skill.

Words.—Rising—ardour. Drooping—fatalism. Widely spaced—extravagance. Getting smaller—skill, irony. Getting bigger—confidence. Connected together—assimilation, calculation. Many to the line—economy, avarice. Few to the line—generosity. Without end letters—reserve, economy.

Letters.—With hooks—egotism, pride. Angular—personality. Rounded—egotism. Disconnected—extravagance. Well proportioned—taste, poetry. Disguised in themselves—cunning hypocrisy. Disproportioned—lack of judgment. Close together—avarice. Weak and pointed—lack of resolution. Closed—reserve, lies. Last letters angular—obstinacy. Illegible—bizarre character. Very faint—weakness. Unequal downstrokes—versatility. Downstrokes disconnected—disorder. Open—candour, gossip. Wide—imagination. Very heavy—pose.

Capitals.—Lower than the line—lack of taste. Too high—meanness. Large—pride. Small—simplicity. Put instead of small letters—pride, egotism. Harmonious—restraint, justness, taste.

Curves.—Exaggerated—imagination. Firm—daring. Soft—laziness. Numerous—kindness, gentleness.

Hooks.—On the capitals—egotism. Backward—egotism. Very marked—pride.

Dashes.—At the end of the lines—doubt, distrust. Hard and broken off—pigheadedness. Getting thicker—strong will. Uncertain—timidity, cunning. Dashing—vivacity, ardour. Dashing upwards—rashness. Supple—kindness, gentleness.

Crossing of the " T."—With angular backstroke—obstinacy. Short and clear—resolution. Hooked—tenacity. Pointed—will-power, no consistence. Club shaped—obstinacy. Serpentine—will-power, suppleness. In mesh—independent. Strong, with sudden stop—limited ideas. Very faint—weak will. Long—vivacity. Missing—lack of will-power. Placed high up—despotism. Long and strong—firmness, energy.

Various.—Numerous angles—cold heart. Angles very acute—obstinacy. End letters hooked—narrowness. End letters long—extravagance, large views. Numerous flourishes—pride. Great movements of the pen—imagination, exaltation. Decorations—self-sufficiency. Small letters printed—artistic sense. Dots missing—imprudence, excessive confidence. No punctuation—thoughtlessness, imprudence. Signs accentuated—intense abilities. Signs irregular—unequal abilities.

VIII

Influences which Modify the Writing

The influences, which are capable of deforming, of altering the nature of the writing, are moral or physical.

They must be taken into account, and it will be seen at once how difficult they make graphological decisions.

It is certain that if one is pressed for time, if at the moment of writing one is in a bad temper, if one has the kind of pen to which one is not used, if one is preoccupied, saddened, or on the other hand enthusiastic, the writing will show it.

Through adopting the official style of writing esteemed by administrations, the bureaucrat will end by losing his spontaneity to some extent. In the same manner monks and nuns, soldiers, school pupils all have a kind of uniform writing due to restraint. But as soon as they are free from this restraint, their individual character reasserts itself.

And then there is the nervous person whose writing gets jumpy (more than it would normally be), the drunkard who makes it shaky, the madman who makes it eccentric, etc.

Certain manual occupations make the hand heavy; on the other hand the liberal professions give a great freedom. Lovers of the æsthetic all have a harmonious writing

Age exerts an influence—the heavy, hesitating and impersonal writing of the child gets lighter, firmer and personal. Towards the age of twenty we generally have a *writing*. On the threshold of old age the writing tends to get less firm and to shake.

The sex of the writer is also generally easily recognised. A woman's writing is usually light, rounded, sloping, with long end letters, very long letters and in the whole thinner than a man's which is firmer, quieter, more connected.

It would take too long to note all the influences which may alter the writing—ink, pen, light, seat, paper, clothes, cold, etc.—and as to the signs of the nationality of the writer, that would lead us too far. Let us merely note that :—

The English writing is usually high, angular, with broken and badly shaped lines.

The German writing is almost always regular, thoughtful, sloping.

The Slav (Russian or other) writing shows in its roundness and disconnection the suppleness of these nations.

The Italian writing is harmonious, artistic, less energetic than the Anglo-Saxon.

IX

Luck and Handwriting

Here is a small table, borrowed from Papus (the *Book of Luck*) which, according with the data of the preceding pages, will show you :—

The signs of good luck (therefore to be sought)—
Lines slanting upwards.
Crossing of the " T " high or upwards.
Letters connected and clear.
Wide margins.
The ' o ' and " a " open.
Dots on the " i " well marked.

The signs of bad luck (therefore to be corrected)—
Lines slanting downwards.
" T " crossing missing, too low or sloping downwards.
Letters disconnected and badly shaped.
Lack of margins.
The " o " and " a " closed.
Dots on the " i " badly marked.

We make our reservations as to the margins, but add :—

To the signs of good luck :—
Round, regular, legible writing.
Writing without backward hooks.
Upright or slightly sloping writing.

To the signs of bad luck :—
Angular, squat or illegible writing.
Writing with backward hooks.
Backward or exaggeratedly sloping writing.

The explanation of this advice is neither occult nor extraordinary. Those who have properly read the present chapter will have noticed that the writing corresponding to the signs of good luck is that of optimistic, intelligent, frank, good persons, not egotistical or hypocritical; that of the unlucky ones being also that of the pessimist, the man without ideas, of weak will-power, insufficient reflection, egotistical, coarse, hypocritical.

And the best means of succeeding in life has always been to have a loyal, firm, generous character, to be confident in one's own power, and not to undertake anything thoughtlessly or without the will to carry through.

X

Types of Handwriting

Serious study of any science will lead to a particular manner of classification. Thus we have seen chiromancers of repute make different groupings of the various forms and styles of hands. In the same way in Graphology Professor Raymond—to mention no others—has divided handwritings into a certain number of types shown by the following table :—

(a) *The plebeian writing.*—Coarse, heavy and gross. It is that of the common people who do not like to hold a pen, and if they are forced to do so, they put into it the coarseness of their mind which thinks little and of their awkward hand.

(b) *The practical writing.*—That of doctors, underwriters, architects, etc. The letters are very harmonious, connected, close, small, often illegible.

(c) *The æsthetic writing.*—Lightly traced, with graceful curves. Letters printed. The writing of musicians generally slopes upwards, harmonious ; that of painters has artistic and somewhat soft curves ; that of sculptors has disconnected letters, that of the actor flourishes, some vanity, a tendency to the fanciful.

(d) *The copybook writing.*—That of the clerk. No idealism. A dry, banal writing.

(e) *The intellectual writing.*—Medium height, moderate slope, calm lines, regular punctuation, signature sloping upwards, the various signs of order, thought and a laudable ambition.

(f) *The writing of genius.*—Superior harmony in a disjointed writing, proof of an intuitive mind and a creative imagination. Simplicity and clearness. No flourishes.

(g) *The mixed writing.*—It is the writing of the soldier, aviator, fencer, etc. Impatience, nervousness, end letters like a whip lash.

GRAPHOLOGY

(*h*) *The rounded writing.*—Gentleness, charm, kindness, sometimes weakness.

(*i*) *The angular writing.*—Gravity, severity, courage, rigidity, sometimes quibbling.

(*j*) *The pathological writing.*—It shows impressive or expressive derangements. It is always odd. It shows itself in various ways :—shaking, sudden bursts, breaks, exaggerations, lines very wavy, etc. The criminal has the signs of falseness and of coarseness, a sinistrogyrous writing, enormous club-shaped letters, etc.

.   .   .   .   .

Another method of classification has been suggested by Dr. Schwiedland, based on the examination of the slopes, which he has divided into six categories :—

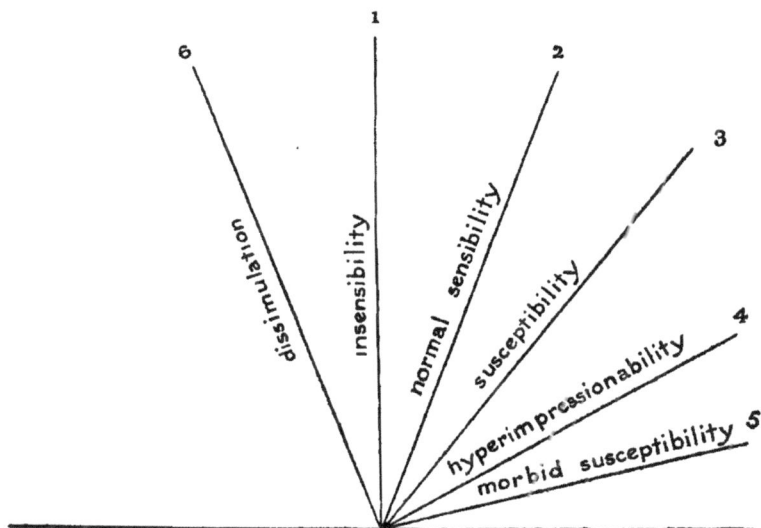

BASIS OF WRITING OF THE SCHWIEDLAND GRAPHOMETER.

Direction 1—vertical—cold and reserved natures.
Direction 2—continued sensitiveness, without passions.
Direction 3—passionate sensitiveness, but governed by will-power.
Direction 4—the will-power diminishes ; sensitiveness gains the victory.
Direction 5—a susceptibility almost diseased.
Direction 6 (to the left of 1)—timidity, dissimulation.